Excel for Beginners 2023

A Comprehensive Excel Guide from Beginners to
Advanced

Warren G. Garcia

ISBN-13: 979-8393753306

DEDICATION

To every one of my readers!

TABLE OF CONTENT

Introduction

Excel is pronounced "Eks - sel", and it is a spreadsheet that functions like a database. It is composed of individual cells which could be used to generate tables, graphs and calculations, that make it easy to analyze and organize huge amounts of data.

This spreadsheet software was built by Microsoft. Excel enables you to carry out mathematical operations and arranges data in rows and columns. iOS, Android, macOS, and Windows are all enabled. The first edition was introduced in 1985 and has undergone many modifications ever since. The basic functionality, however, generally stays the same.

MS Excel is used to store and analyze numerical and statistical data. it has many features that could be used to accomplish various tasks, such as pivot tables, graphing, tools, computations, macro programming, etc.
Excel's biggest advantage is its capacity to be used for a wide range of business operations including finance, forecasting, business intelligence, forecasting, analysis, data management, and statistics.

The few tasks it can perform for you are as follows:
- Store and Import Data
- Manipulating Text
- Templates/Dashboards
- Number Crunching
- Automation of Tasks
- Charts and Graphs
- And Much More…

Chapter 1: What Is Excel?

Excel is a software application created by Microsoft that uses spreadsheets to arrange data and figures via functions and formulas. Excel analysis, which is commonly used worldwide, is employed by organizations of all kinds to handle business analysis. You can use MS Excel to organize, format and evaluate data in a spreadsheet.

Excel is used across all enterprises and organizations from the least to the greatest and it is commonly used to organize and perform financial analysis. The boxes in the Excel program are known as cells, which are organized in columns and rows. These cells are designed to keep data.

What is Excel used for?

Excel is widely used in corporate environments. It is deployed, for instance, in human resource management, performance reporting, business analysis, and operations management. Excel leverages on a significant number of organized cells to setup and modify data as well as do arithmetic operations. Using pivot tables, and graphing tools, and formulas, you can organize data in the spreadsheet.

MS Excel is often used by companies for the following things:
- Data entry and storage;
- Office administration,
- Data analysis;
- Strategic analysis;
- Accounting and budgeting;
- Performance reporting;
- Project management;
- Collection and verification of business data;
- Business analysis;
- Administrative and managerial management.

Terminologies Used in Excel

Excel's terminology for its components may not be easily comprehensible to new subscribers. Yet, these terms will become simpler over time and with consistent use. Listed below are some of the terminologies used in Excel:

Cell
A cell, this is where a row and a column connect, it is also the section for data inputs

Cell Reference
These refer to the values that identify a cell's location. While, rows are horizontal and numbered, columns are vertical and designated with a letter.

Active Cell
A green box that indicates which cell is currently selected.

Workbook
The Excel workbook comprises one or even more worksheets.

Worksheet
These are various files that constitute a Workbook.

Worksheet tab
These include the tabs on the spreadsheet's bottom left.

Row and Column Headings
These are cells with letters and numbers that are placed near to the borders of the rows and columns. When a header is selected, the total column or row is outlined.

Formula
A set of instructions that Excel must execute.

Formula bar
This is an extended entry area used to enter data or formulas into cells. It is sited right next to the "fx" label on the top of the worksheet.

Address bar
This bar, which may be seen to the left of the formula bar, shows the letter and numeric location of a cell that is active.

Filter
These guidelines could be used to determine which worksheet rows to display. On the right-hand corner of the home bar, below it, you can use this feature by clicking "Sort & Filter". If the auto filter option is enabled, only the rows that match unique values will be shown.

AutoFill

Using this component will make copying data to various cells convenient. In order to instantly fill up the blank cells in a series of two or more cells, Drag the mouse pointer over the cell's bottom right corner and hold it until a black + sign shows. Drag the + icon over the cells you need to fill in while clicking and pressing down the left mouse button. Then, the AutoFill feature automatically completes the series for you.

AutoSum

You can add various numbers with the help of this function. You can click the Alt and Equal keys when choosing the cells to add and also, there is a button to switch on this option in the upper right-hand corner of the home page, right above "Fill" and next to "Sort & Filter."

PivotTable

This data summation device instantly arranges and evaluates data. This can be seen on the extreme left, below the insert tab.

PivotChart

This chart offers graph visualizations of the data as a pictorial help.

Excel's Complex Functions

The following Excel tools are more complex:

TREND Feature

Using a collection of Y or X values, this function calculates linear trend lines. It can be used to forecast future trends or time series trend analysis. Charts can use trendlines.

VLOOKUP

The VLOOKUP operation, which searches for numbers in a large data set, can be used to export the data into a new table. This cell input command VLOOKUP shows as =VLOOKUP (). You can define an estimated or precise result by stating True or False in the bracket together with the data they are searching for, where to look for it, and the column number containing the value to return.

Table Array

This is the aggregation of two or more tables containing connected and correlated data and values.

Col_ index Num

Col_index num is an integer that indicates the column in the provided table array that you want to obtain a value from

HB Range

A colon which is used to indicate a set of cells or tables between the first and last cell.

MIX and MIN Functions

Minimum and Maximum values from specific data sets are given by these functions. Inside this function tab, MAX is used to determine the highest value, while MIN is used to get the lowest value.

AND Function

When seeking value, this feature has many metrics in place. A value's result will be given back as true provided it meets the requirement; else, it will be given back as false. The function's input must match this: =AND (logical1, [logical2],).

The Future of Excel

What is the next step for us? It is reasonable that the desires of many will triumph because the online space is such a crucial part of our businesses and lives. Sustaining existing knowledge of cutting-edge technology is becoming a full-time task as the Microsoft platforms continue to advance. Excel will continue to be the ideal software for creating charts, analyzing data, making presentations, and connecting with strong tools for BI workflows and visual dashboards.

Businesses are adopting cloud computing to a greater extent due to the collaboration and data's accessibility. In this space, we predict MS Excel's advancement to take up momentum over the years ahead, allowing multi-user entry to large data sets for reporting, analysis and significantly improved productivity.

Basics of Cell

Users will continually enter content—or data—into cells while working with Excel. The core components of a worksheet are cells. To arrange, analyze and compute data in Excel, you will have to know the foundations of cells and cell content.

Cells are the countless number of rectangles that constitute each worksheet. A cell is the area where a column and a row connect, or between column and a row.

Numbers are used to identify rows (3,4,5) while letters are used to identify columns (C, D, E). According to its row and column, every cell has a specific name, commonly called a cell address.

For instance, if a selected cell meets at column D and row 4, then the cell address is called D4

However, it is allowed to choose many cells simultaneously. A cell range is a set of cells. Users can relate to a cell range by using cell addresses of both the first and last cells in the range, separated by a colon, instead of a single cell address. Cells C1, C2, C3, C4, and C5 would be part of the range denoted by the letters C1:C5. Look at the several cells ranges below:

Cell range C1:C6
cell range C1:C6

Cell range D1:D4
cell range D1:D4

Cell range E2:E7
cell range E2:E7

When Selecting a Cell

To choose a cell, click on it; for example, let us pick cell C3.

The row and column headings will be outlined, and a border would display around the chosen cell. Unless you pick another cell in the worksheet, the highlighted cell will stay highlighted.

The arrow buttons on your keyboard can also be employed to select cells.

To Select a Cell Range

When all of the neighboring cells you want to choose are marked, click and drag the mouse over cells. In this case, let's choose the cells C5–D10.

To pick the appropriate cell range, let go of the mouse. Unless you pick another cell in the worksheet, the highlighted cells will remain selected.

The selected cell range is C5:D10

Cell Content

Every bit of data you enter in a spreadsheet is saved in a cell. Formatting, text, formulae and functions are only a few examples of the various content forms that can be included in a cell.

Text

Text, such as words, dates, and numbers can be included in cells.

Formatting Options

Formatting attributes enable you to alter how dates, numbers, and letters are shown in cells. Instances of percentages could be 15% or 0.15%. You can even modify the background color or text of a cell.

Formulas and Functions: Functions and formulae that estimate cell values are located in cells. SUM (C3:C6) for example adds the values of all the cells in the C3:C6 range and shows the result in cell C7.

To Insert Content in A Cell

To choose a cell, click on it. In this case, let's choose cell D8.
Input the text you would like to insert into the selected cell after entering it. The formula bar and the cell will show the data. In the formula bar, you can input and change cell content.

How to Clear (or Delete) Cell Content

Pick the cell(s) containing the information you want to remove. In this case, let's choose the cells C3:F8.

Press the Home tab's Clear command, then select "Clear Contents". The details of the cell will be deleted.

Users could also erase content from various cells simultaneously by using the Delete button on the keyboard. Only a cell can be removed at a time using the Backspace key.

To Delete Cells

There is a crucial distinction between removing a cell's content and the main cell. Whenever a cell is erased in its totality, the cells underneath it will migrate to fill in the areas left by the erased cells.

Copying And Pasting Cell Content

Excel provides you the choice to copy and paste information that has previously been typed in your spreadsheet into other cells, this can spare you effort and time.

click the Delete command on the home tab of the ribbon.

The cells under will go upwards and fill in the spaces.

Pick the cell or cells you like to copy. In this case, let's use D5.

From your keyboard, click Ctrl+C or press the Copy menu on the Home tab.

To paste the content into the cells, pick the cell or cells. In this example, let's pick D7:D11. There should be a dashed box enclosing the replicated cell or cells.

Simply enter Ctrl+V on your keyboard or choose the paste option on the home tab

The data will be pasted in the cells that have been picked.

Many other paste options are also accessible, which are useful when dealing with cells that have formatting or formulae. To access these alternatives, simply click the drop-down icon on the Paste command.

Formulas And Functions

In Excel, calculations can be expressed through formulas and functions. Formulas are defined instructions for working out calculations.

In any approach, all functions and formulas should start with an equal sign ('=') and be put in a cell.

A formula contains the addresses of the cells in which values will be altered just after the equal sign, with the appropriate operands inserted in between. Common arithmetic operators are employed as the operands:

Addition
Addition uses the "+" operator;
for instance, = A5+A7

Subtraction
Subtraction uses the -operator;
for instance, = A9-A3

Division
Division uses / operator
For instance, = A6/A3

Multiplication
Multiplication uses * operator
For instance, = A8*A4

Exponential
Exponential uses the ^ operator
For instance, = A5^A2

Enter A Formula
Follow the procedure to input a formula.
- Pick a cell.
- Type an equal (=) symbol to tell Excel that you intend to add a formula.
  For instance, type the formula A2+A6.

Rather than entering A2 and A6, just pick cells A2 and A6.
The value of cell A1 should be changed to A3.

Recalculation
Cell A3's value is recalculated by Excel instantly. This is also one of Excel's most essential operations.

Edit A Formula

When a cell is chosen, Excel displays its formula or value within the formula bar.

Formula Bar

To modify a formula,
- Click in the formula bar and perform any needed modifications.
- Click Enter.

Press Operator Precedent

Calculations in Excel are done in a particular order. A formula's parentheses specify which part of the equation should be calculated first. Thereafter calculations for division or multiplication are done. When this is done, Excel will proceed to Subtract and add from your formula.

Copy/Paste A Formula

When a formula is copied, Excel auto updates the cell references for every new cell the duplicated formula is inserted into. To comprehend it better, follow these procedures.

- Enter these formulae into a cell A5, A2+A3

- Right-click on cell A5 then select Copy in the menu that displays (or press CTRL + C)

- Now, choose the Paste icon under "Paste Options" after choosing cell B5 using the right click of the mouse (or press CTRL + v).

- Furthermore, you could drag the formula into cell B5. select cell A5 by positioning your cursor in its lower right corner, and after that drag it to cell B5. This is much simpler and delivers the same output.

Insert Function

The design of every function remains the same. E.g., SUM (B2:B5). This function is known as SUM.

The term "arguments" implies that we are providing Excel the range B2:B5 as an entry. The data in cells B2, B3, B4, and B5 are added by this function. Knowing what argument to use and what function to use for each task is hard. Excel's Insert Function option fortunately enables you with this.

You can use these steps to add a function.
- Select a cell.
- Choose the Insert Function button.
- Select a function from the section or search for the function. Select COUNTIF, for instance, in the Statistical category.
- Select Ok

A dialog box for "Function Arguments" shows.
- Pick the range B1:D2 by selecting it in the Range box.
- Select the criteria box and enter >
- select ok

Function Arguments Dialog Box
The result shows the COUNTIF function evaluates the number of cells that are higher than five.

Financial and Accounting Uses

MS Office Excel was designed to handle accounting tasks such as creating balance sheets, budgeting, and financial statements. It has various features for handling challenging mathematical operations in addition to basic spreadsheet functions. You can export and import financial and banking data to and from various accounting program platforms, and it allows a broad range of add-ons for operations like financial forecasting and modeling. It also makes it easy to interface with external data.

Budgeting And Statements

One of the core elementary accounting files is a profit and loss statement, and it is one of the templates provided in Microsoft Office Excel. Also, you can get specialized templates from any outside suppliers and install them in the software, or you could get more complicated statements and budgeting templates from the Microsoft site. If you need to construct distinctive or advanced budgets or financial statements, you could either build one from the start using Excel's features or edit a pre-existing template and make use of its components.

Spreadsheets

Excel spreadsheets are built to hold data in a tabular form that permits summation and in-inline calculations, reducing the need for specialized accounting calculators and ticker tape. Line calculations are a primary accounting operation. Excel can perform summation and simple calculations more conveniently than an accounting calculator because the content in the spreadsheet is storable and reusable. Through making graphs and charts from the spreadsheet data, you will have access to a variety of media and several different components of the same data. Furthermore, add-ons can be applied to explore the data, construct, and generate financial projections.

External Data

Excel enables you to import data through a diverse range of sources. Accounting can gain significantly from this because you can collect bank information, sales data and invoices, from different sources into a single central spreadsheet to aid your accounting operations. You can get data from various sections of your organization without doing extra data entry since the data can be saved in many databases and file types prior to getting imported.

Integration

So many known accounting application programs enable Excel integration. To connect Excel spreadsheets to your accounting information, in this case, you can use the wizards that exist with your chosen accounting application program. This will enable you to conduct pull and push data operations via Excel and your accounting application program on request.

Chapter 2: Why Learn Excel in 2022?

Excel is widely used in enterprises and industries presently to manage and save data. You can arrange any form of data and information with Excel. MS Excel is the best spreadsheet program in the world, and anyone who understands how to use it can benefit greatly from it.
Listed below are the benefits of Microsoft Excel.

- MS Excel Efficiently stores data
- Excel is suitable for mobile and internet usage.
- Excel offers all the full collection of data analysis tools.
- Excel makes Printing reports simple
- Saves data with a lot of rows.
- You can automate via code in MS excel
- Excel Clean up and modify data
- There are numerous free designs to use
- Excel makes it simple in using Charts to Produce Data Visualizations
- MS excel enable you to perform calculations

Why Use Formulas?

Excel Formulas
Formula in MS Excel is an operation that transforms values in a group of cells. Even though the answer is wrong, these formulas nevertheless yield a result. You can do calculations like subtraction, division, multiplication, and addition with Excel formulae. MS Excel also enables one to work with time and date values, determine percentages and averages for a range of cells, and execute a lot of things.
To execute mathematical operations, an Excel formula is employed. An equal sign (=) and your calculations are entered in the cell at the beginning of a formula.

These types of calculations can be performed via formulas:

- Addition
  = 3+4
- Multiplication
  = 5*2
- Division
  = 6/3

How To Add Text to A Cell in Excel?

Adding text in Excel

We could immediately insert text into a range of chosen cells in the worktable through the Excel add text to cell function. Within our chosen cell range, just add a prefix, a suffix, a string, or any other elements that you need.

In Excel, we might periodically have to add specialized or general text at the outset or end of a selection of cells. We can also indicate the actual position of the input in Excel. This could take a long time to enter the text into each cell manually.

By using the ampersand (&) formula, we can simply enter text into an Excel.

What Is Multiply Formula in Excel?

MS Excel has no designed multiplication formula but, Multiplication in excel is done by inputting the "equal to"(=) sign, then the first number, thereafter the "asterisk" (*), and lastly the second number.

For instance, the formula "=4*5*2" multiplies the numbers 4, 5, and 3 which gives 60 in return.

The multiplicand is the number which is to be multiplied, while the multiplier is the number by which the multiplicand is multiplied. Both multiplicand and multiplier are also known as Factors.

The result or the outcome of the multiplication is known as the product.

Multiplication in Excel could be done in the following way

Using the PRODUCT function

Using the "asterisk" symbol (*)

Using the SUMPRODUCT function

N.B: The SUMPRODUCT function multiplies and then sums the resulting products.

IF Functions of Excel

IF function

One of the commonly used functions in Excel is the IF function, which permits you to evaluate values logically to expectations.

Hence, an IF statement yields two outcomes. If your comparison is True, then you get the first result; but if it's False, you get the second result.

E.g., =IF(D3="Yes",2,3) says IF(D3=Yes, then return a 2, if not return a 3).

Simple IF examples
Cell F3 contains a formula =IF(H2="Yes",1,2)
=IF(H2="Yes",1,2)
Cell F3 in this example reads: "IF (H2 = Yes, then return a 1, else return a 2)."

Cell A3 contains the formula =IF(B3=1,"YES","NO")
=IF(B=3,"Yes","No")
In this instance, cell A3's formula reads: IF (If B3=1, return Yes; else, return No).

As you can see, one could evaluate value and text with the IF function. Error detection is another potential of the IF Function.
You have many options beyond just evaluating two things to determine if they are equal and giving one answer; you could also apply mathematical operators and do extra computations in line with your criteria. Moreover, you can merge many IF functions in order to perform different comparisons.

Guidelines And Examples of Array Formulas.

An array formula is a formula that can perform various calculations on one or more components of an array. An array could be viewed as a row, column, or collection of both rows and columns of values. Array formulas may generate one outcome or a number of outcomes.

Array formula can be employed to perform a tedious task like:
- To add up every Nth value in a range of values
- Simply adding the figures that match the requirements to the total, such as the lowest values in a figure or ranges that fall between a lower and upper border.
- To quickly prepare sample datasets.
- Estimating how many characters can be found in a group of cells.

For example
Let's say you are interested in obtaining the total sales figure for a set of items in column B with costs in column C.
Of course, nothing is stopping you from first determining the subtotals in each row via a formula like =B3*D3 and then summing the outcomes:
But, because an array formula tells Excel to save intermediate outcomes in memory rather than in an additional column, you could bypass those extra

keystrokes. And hence, all it needed are 2 short steps and a one array formula:

1 Choose a vacant cell, after which insert the formula into it:
=SUM(C2:C6*D2:D6)
To finalize the array formula, click CTRL + SHIFT + ENTER on your keyboard.
Immediately you do this, MS Excel puts "curly brackets {}" all around the formula, which serves as a visual reference that it is an array formula.
What the formula does is to multiply the values in each individual row of the specified array (cells C3 through D7), add the subtotals together, and output the grand total:
The formula multiplies the values in each row of the selected array, that is (cells B2 through C6), and adds the respective subtotals, and returns the entire sum:

Average Formula in Excel

How To Calculate Averages in Excel

Averages come in a broad range of forms, and there are many procedures to calculate them.

1. AVERAGE
2. AVERAGEA
3. AVERAGEIF
4. MEDIAN
5. MODE

1. AVERAGE

The arithmetic mean is the commonly known average, and MS Excel uses the AVERAGE function to find it. An average value can be created from a distribution, list of data or range by using the Excel AVERAGE function. It is determined by adding up all of the list's numbers, subsequently dividing the outcome by the number of values there are in the list.

Excel's AVERAGE function is easy, having this syntax:
=AVERAGE(number2, [number3],...)
You could make use of cell references or ranges instead of specified values. The AVERAGE function can handle up to 255 arguments, each of which can be a cell reference, a range, or a value. Though only one argument is needed, the AVERAGE function mostly certainly requires at least two.

The formula below will calculate the average of the numbers 60, 35, and 50.
=AVERAGE(60,35,50)

To calculate the average of values in cells C2, C3, C4, and C5 enter:
=AVERAGE(C2:C5)
It can also be chosen on the worksheet by selecting the first cell in the range and moving the mouse to the last cell in the range. This can be inserted directly into the cell or formula bar.
Just press down the Control (or Command for Mac users) key when performing your selections to calculate the average of non-contiguous (non-adjacent) cells.
Non-contiguous references are separated by commas if inserted simply into the cell or formula bar.

2. AVERAGEA

This function computes the average of a given set of data.

In contrast to the AVERAGE function, it analyzes text-based numerals and logical values TRUE and FALSE. AVERAGE just excludes these values during calculation.

Formula

=AVERAGEA(value1, [value2], …)

Where:

A required argument is Value1. Notwithstanding, the remaining values are not needed.

Values that are given can be ranges, cell references named ranges, or numbers. There can be 255 arguments provided.

3. AVERAGEIF

There are approaches for computing the average using only the values that meet particular criteria. Excel determines the arithmetic mean of the cells that meet a specific criterion by looking within the defined range for the AVERAGEIF function.

The syntax of the AVERAGEIF function is:

=AVERAGEIF(range, criteria,[average_range])

The range is the region where we can predict the location of cell that meet the condition

The expression or value that Excel would check for within a given range is the condition.

The average range is an optional argument The data to be averaged are situated in this group of cells. The range is used when the average range is left out.

AVERAGEIF example 1

For instance, we can tell Excel to exclusively select the cells that have "apples" in column B and determine their average cost in column C from a list that contains numerous fruit prices.

AVERAGEIF example 2

As shown in the given example, the condition in an AVERAGEIF function could also be expressed in the format of a logical expression:

=AVERAGEIF(C4:G4,"< >0")

The average of the values between C4 to G4 which are not equal to zero would be determined through the use of the formula given above. Take note that the third (optional) argument is left out, the range's cells are used to calculate the average.

4. MEDIAN

The middle number in a collection of numbers is known as the median.

The syntax is:

=MEDIAN(number1, [number2], …)

Rather than employing explicit values, you can also make use of cell references or ranges.

In the case below, the numerical sequence would be:

5,10,11,12,14,15,15,16,17,23,28,31,200.

The distribution includes 13 numbers, making the seventh one the middle number. So, 15 is the median.

Taking the average of the two numbers in the center of a distribution for an even number of values would give the median. The median of these given numbers 3,5,11,13,13,17, would be (11+13)/2=12.

Text, logical values, and empty cells are not considered when calculating the MEDIAN function.

    5.   MODE

The third way to calculate the average value of a number set is to determine the mode, or the value that returns the most frequently.

Excel currently offers three "mode" features. MODE, the classic, follow the syntax of:

=MODE(number1, [number2],...)

Using this function, Excel examines the numbers in the range or list and selects the value that occurs the most frequently to represent the average for the set.

Nevertheless, there are instances when more than one number could be taken as the mode. Look at the following list, for instance:

5, 12, 15, 17,17,18, 19, 19, 21, 23, 23, 28, 200

Every of the figures 17, 19, and 23 occurs twice. Which is the mode? Microsoft takes the first value that shows as the mode, which in our instance above is 17.

Based on which number came within the distribution first, Excel will select among the numbers 17, 19, and 23 when the numbers are put in a random order.

For example, in the list:

5,17,21,17,23,28,200,23,19,15,18,19,12

The MODE function considers 17 as the mode.

Basic Excel Percentage Formula

This is the core Excel formula for calculating percentages:

Percentage = Part/Total

You'll realize that Excel's % calculation doesn't include the *100 portions compared to the basic mathematical formula for percentage. Excel automatically multiplied the resultant fraction by 100 when the Percentage style is applied to a cell, so you have no need to do this manually when calculating a percentage.

Let's now analyze how to apply the Excel percentage formula to actual data. Given that column B shows the number of "Ordered things" and column D shows the number of "Delivered items." Use these methods to calculate the percentage of delivered products:

Input the equation =D2/B2 in cell E2 and repeat it across many rows as desired.

To show the resultant decimal fractions as percentages, choose the % Sign button (Home tab > Number group).

The same sequence of steps shall be performed when using any other percentage formula in Excel.

How Do You Calculate Variance in Excel?

Variance is a measurement of the variation of values within a data collection. Variance determines how much farther apart from the mean every number in the set is. To evaluate the variance of the data you have inputted into a spreadsheet, make use of Microsoft Excel.

H3 How to Calculate Variance in Excel

In order to determine the variance, you must have inputted your data set into Excel. After you've gathered your data, depending on the kind of set of data you acquire and the type of variation you need to calculate, you can select a formula.

The formula in Excel has many unique variations for calculating variance:

=VAR.P(select data)

=VARA(select data)

=VAR.S(select data)

You would select the cell range you would like to apply after the brackets for each of the formulas. Use =VAR.S (C3:C9) in this case to determine the variance, for the data in cells C3 through C4.

For Excel to detect that you're inputting a formula, you must commence with the "=" sign.

In order to decide on the right formula to use, it is necessary to understand the kind of data you are dealing with. For instance, when any text values are included in the data set, VARA will take them as 0, FALSE as 0, and true as 1, while VAR.S excludes any values apart from numeric values. This would alter how your variance calculations come out.

VAR.P, on the contrary, utilizes the whole data collection to measure the variance in a population. VAR.S can be applied in your calculation if you don't have access to all of the data for the population.

Generally, VAR.S is the Excel formula that is being use most regularly to determine variance

Excel Profit Chart

How to Build a Chart in Excel

MS Excel is widely used by professionals as well as businesses to determine financial returns and earning, but individuals also can produce chart visualizations that support the data companies provided quarterly and the annual financial statistics given to analysts, shareholders and external and internal stakeholders, such as suppliers and employees. Therefore, to make business decisions, these professionals use this unprocessed data. Your business data presentation ought to have a concise and interesting narrative. A chart is an excellent visual means of conveying possibly lifeless messages and numerical concepts.

Chapter 3: What Are Excel Formulas?

Excel formulas enable you to do calculations on the numbers present in your spreadsheet's cells, display the outcomes in the cell of your choice, and discover links between these values.

A formula in Excel is an operation that alters values in a range of cells or in a cell. Take for instance the formula =C1+C2+C3, which estimates the sum of the values in cells C1 through C3.

The follow are the basic formulae in Excel:
SUM
AVERAGE
COUNT
COUNTA
IF
TRIM
MIN MAX

Five Times-Saving Ways to Insert Formula into Excel

1. Simple insertion: Entering a formula in the cell

The easiest way to input basic Excel formulas is by entering them into a formula bar or a cell and this method begins with the equal sign, and then the name of an Excel function.

2. Employing the Insert Function icon on the Formulas tab

You only need to make use of the Excel Insert Function dialog box to gain absolute control over the insertion of your function. To accomplish this, click the Formulas tab and then choose the Insert Function option in the 1st menu. All the features you needed to finish your financial analysis is accessible in the dialogue box

3. Choose a Formula from a Group in the Formula Tab

This approach is for persons who want to swiftly learn their favorite features. Go to the Formulas tab and then choose your selected group to access this menu. A submenu displaying a list of functions will show when you click it.

4. AutoSum Option usage

You can always apply the AutoSum feature for fast and day to day activities, simply locate the Formulas tab and select the AutoSum icon. Afterwards, click the caret to display any additional hidden formulas. The Home tab also gives this option.

5. Quick Insert: Make use of the most recent tabs

Employ the Recently Used selection if entering in the most current formula continually overwhelms you. It can be located on the Formulas tab, as the 3rd menu option next to AutoSum.

Simple Excel Formulas for Workflow

Let's check some fundamental Excel functions for your workflow.

1. **SUM**

The first Excel formula you ought to know is the SUM function. Generally, it combines values across many rows or columns inside the range that was chosen.

2. **AVERAGE**

The AVERAGE function should recall you back to the basic averages of data, such as the average number of shareholders in a certain shareholding pool.

3. **COUNT**

Count function enumerates all cells in a specific range that contains numerical values only.

4. **COUNTA**

Like the COUNT function, the COUNTA function enumerates every cell in a given range. However, it counts every cell, irrespective of cell type. In other words, it counts times, empty strings, dates, strings, logical value and text in addition to numbers, unlike COUNT, which only enumerates numbers.

5. **IF**

Whenever you need to organize your data depending on a particular logic, the IF function is commonly used. The ability to incorporate functions and formulas is the unique part of the IF formula.

6. **TRIM**

The TRIM function makes sure that extra spaces in your data did not cause the functions to output errors, by making sure there are no any open spots. TRIM solely works on just a single cell, unlike all the other functions that can work on a wide range of cells. The consequence is that it has the problem of loading your spreadsheet with duplicated data.

7. **MIN & MAX**

The MAX and MIN functions help to identify the lowest and highest value within a range of numbers.

Sum

SUM function
Values are added by SUM function. cell references, Individual values ranges, or a combination of every one of them can be added.
For instance:

=SUM(B2:B10) implies that the values in the cells B2:B10 should be added.

=SUM(B2:B10, D2:D10) implies that the values in the cells B2:B10, as well as the cells in D2:D10 should be added

Average

In Excel, this would give the average value of the provided collection of numbers. The function is employed to determine the arithmetic mean of a set of inputs.

Formula=AVERAGE(number1, [number2], …)
The following arguments are used by the function:
Number1 (required argument) – This is the first figure of the range or cell reference for determining the average.
Number2 (optional argument) – They are the extra figures, a range or cell reference for which we need to determine the average. A max of 255 numbers is permitted.

COUNT

The COUNT function counts the number of numeric values in each cell along with the number of numerical values present inside the list of arguments. To find out the number of inputs in a number field which is within an array or range of numbers, apply the COUNT function. To determine how many numbers are in the range B1:B15, for instance, apply the formula =COUNT (B1:B15). In this instance, the output will be 3 if three of the range's cells include numbers.

COUNTA

The COUNTA function counts the cells in a range that are not blank.
Syntax
COUNTA(value1, [value2], ...)

IF

One of the most commonly used functions in Excel is the IF function, which permits comparing of values logically to what is anticipated.
Thus, an IF expression can yield two outcomes. If your comparison is True, then the first result is what you get; if it's False, you get the second.
For instance, =IF(A3="Yes",1,2) says IF(A3 = Yes, then return a 1, otherwise return a 2).

TRIM Function

The customized TRIM function in Excel is used to eliminate uneven text spacing and keep single word spacing.
Unwanted space that can occur before, after, or between numbers or text in a cell is called irregular spacing in a dataset.
It is written =TRIM
Write: if you simply intend on employing the function on one cell:
=TRIM(cell)

Write: if you would like to apply the function to a collection of cells.
=TRIM(start cell:end cell)

Excel Shortcuts

Excel has some set of shortcuts that enable you to swiftly accomplish a given task. Few keyboard strokes can enable you to perform different tasks easily.

Excel Shortcuts

1. To access the View tab
    Alt + W

2. To navigate to the Data tab.
    Alt + A

3. To store a spreadsheet or a workbook
   Ctrl + S

4. To close the open worksheet
   Ctrl + W

5. To delete a cell comment
   Shift + F10 + D

6. To close Excel
   Ctrl + F4

7. To go to the previous sheet
   Ctrl + PageUp

8. To add a comment to a cell
   Shift + F2

9. To copy and paste cells
   Ctrl + C, Ctrl + V

10. To proceed to the subsequent sheet
    Ctrl + PageDown

11. To fill color
    Alt + H + H

12. To center align cell contents
    Alt + H + A + C

13. To italicize and make the font bold
    Ctrl + I, Ctrl + B

14. To select all the cells on the left
    Ctrl + Shift + Left Arrow
15. To view the Formula tab
    Alt + M

16. To edit a cell
    F2

17. To view a recent workbook
    Ctrl + O

18. To make a fresh workbook
Ctrl + N

19. To select the column from the selected cell to the end of the table
Ctrl + Shift + Down Arrow

20. To select all the cells on the right
Ctrl + Shift + Right arrow

Why Use Excel Shortcuts

Why use Excel Shortcuts?
Employing Excel shortcuts, or shortcut keys, is an oftentimes ignored means of improving efficiency when dealing with an Excel model. When applied in place of clicking on the toolbar, these shortcut keys perform significant operations that greatly increase performance and speed.
These shortcuts can accomplish a vast range of operations, from simple spreadsheet navigating to data grouping and formulas filling.

Chapter 4: Modifying the Worksheet

A worksheet in Excel is a single page or sheet found within a workbook, and the workbook is the main Excel file.

The worksheet is also known as the spreadsheet.

The worksheet tabs are located at the bottom of the page. By clicking on this tab, you can reach the page of your workbook. You can modify the worksheet title, add a color fill to the tab, add fresh worksheets, erase them, and also add more worksheets.

To Modifying a Worksheet

- Navigate to the model where the worksheet is.
- Simply select the Worksheets tab.
- You can choose the worksheet's name using the drop-down list.
- Click on select

You Can Carry Out the Following Activities Within a Worksheet

- To delete a column, click its name and then select Delete.
- To move a row, click its link and then choose its new spot from the drop-down menu of rows.
- A column can be moved by clicking its name and selecting its new space from the drop-down list of columns.
- To add a different column, click New Column and choose the property from the drop-down list.
- To clear a row, click its link and then choose Delete.
- Set up a fresh row or rows by clicking New Row and thereafter choose the proper option items or option class.
- A column can be moved by clicking its name and selecting its new spot from the drop-down list of columns.
- Alter the worksheet's name via clicking the present name and entering a different

Moving To a Specific Cell

When searching for a specific cell, such as cell A1, on a broad worksheet, you ordinarily have to navigate the page until the cell A1 shows, which could be time wasting. There is a quick way in which the cell can be selected.

- **By using shortcuts, you can jump to a particular cell.**
Holding down the Ctrl key while pressing Home will cause the cursor to immediately jump to the targeted cell from anywhere on the sheet.
- **Jump to particular cell by box name**
If you need to move to a specific cell, such as B7, you can input the cell reference in the Name box, located to the left of the formula bar, and then click enter key.
- **Employing the Go To function, jump to a specific cell**
To open the Go To dialog, use the F5 key. Type the cell reference you want to move into the Reference textbox, then click OK. The cursor will then jump to the cell you choose

Add A Row

Delete or input a row
Go to Home > Insert > Insert Sheet Rows or Remove Sheet Rows just after choosing any cell in the row.
Another approach is to right-click the row number and choose either Delete or Insert.

Adding The Column

Add or remove a column
Go to Home > Insert > Insert Sheet Columns or Delete Sheet Columns just after choosing any cell in the column.
You could also right-click the column's header and then choose Delete or insert.

How To Resize a Column

Columns Resizing
Choose one column or a set of columns.
choose the Format > Column Width from either the Home menu (or Column Height).
Resize all rows and columns to suit the data instantly.
Choose "Select All" from the dropdown. To choose all rows and columns, choose All at the worksheet's top.

Click on a border twice. To make the data fit, all rows and columns are resized.

Resize a Row
To make the data fit, you can either modify its row height or column width or automatically resize the columns and rows.
Resize rows
Choose a set row or a row.
Choose Format > Row Width in the Home menu (or Row Height).
Choose OK after entering the row width

Selecting a Cell
You can choose the contents between one or more cells, columns, or rows in Excel.
Choosing one or more cells
To select a particular cell, click on it.
When choosing a range, choose a cell first, then use the left mouse button press and drag it over other cells.
You can likewise select the range using Shift + arrow keys.
Hold Ctrl when choosing the cells, it allows you to choose cell ranges and non-adjacent cells.

Choose one or many rows and columns.

To choose an entire column, select the letter at the top. Rather, click any column cell, and after that press Ctrl + Space.

To choose a whole row, choose the row number. Rather, you can click Shift + Space after choosing a cell in the row.
Pressing Ctrl when choosing the column or row numbers enables you to choose non-adjacent columns or rows.

Cutting, Copying and Pasting Cells

Move or Copy Cells and Cell Contents
To copy or move the elements of a cell, use Copy, Paste, and cut. or replicate specific cell elements or attributes. You can, for instance, copy a formula's result value only or you could copy the formula itself.
With Excel, you can drag and drop cells to move it or make use of the Cut and Paste commands.
Choose those cells you would like to copy or move, or a set of them.
Point towards the selection's boundary.
Drag the cell or set of cells to a new area once the pointer turns to a move pointer.

Cells could be moved by applying Cut and Paste.
choose a cell set or a cell.
Press Ctrl + X or choose Home > Cut.
The cell you want to move, the data should be selected

Press Ctrl V or Choose home > Paste
Using Copy and Paste, copy cells
Choose a set of cells or the cell.
Press Ctrl + C or rather choose Copy.
Press Ctrl + V or rather Select Paste.

Keeping Heading Visible

Excel Freeze Panes: Retain Visibility of Row and Column Headings
It's useful to keep the headings for your rows and/or columns visible as you move across the spreadsheet when dealing with a big spreadsheet. A Freeze Panes icon will show up when you choose the View tab on the ribbon and 3 options come up when you click it. Among the three, the first is the most versatile. Once you choose Freeze Panes, the rows above and to the left of the currently specified cell will be frozen to function as headings. No matter how far you move down or to the right, they will remain on the screen. Freeze Top Row and Freeze First Column are the remaining two options, and they operate as expected. As a result, you can instantly freeze any one without worrying about where your cursor is. Selecting one of these options will overrule any prior settings and implement your latest choice. So, you must apply the Freeze Panes option if you need to freeze both rows and columns.

Choose Unfreeze Panes from the Freeze Panes icon on the View tab to turn off Freeze Panes. Stop

Chapter 5: Five ways Excel Can Improve Productivity During Your Work from Home

Using The Fill Handles
The rectangle in the bottom-right area of each Excel selection is the fill handle. Since you don't have to get to the table's bottom, the fill handles are significantly faster.

Evaluating Formulas All at Once
Excel will always present the formula rather than its outcome whenever you edit a cell with a formula. If you want to view each of the formulas on a worksheet simultaneously, you may apply the keyboard shortcut "Control + ~". This shortcut enables you to rapidly modify as many formulas as you want.

Employ the Goal-Seeking Formula
A built-in Excel feature known as Goal Seek allows you to examine how each data point in a formula influence another. You can instantly alter just one cell entry to view the output, making this an efficient tool for "what if" questioning. Since you are able to observe how predictions could vary if one factor is altered, it is very beneficial in sales, forecasting instances and finance. Just choose "What If Analysis" and "Goal Seek" on a cell to get started.

Automate Recurring Operations Via VBA
Visual Basic of Applications (VBA) is one of the essential features in Excel. If you're accustomed to hours of manual data entry, this easy macro helps you to streamline repetitive tasks such that VBA could reduce it to just a few minutes. This can save you a lot of time and be beneficial when working from home or the workplace.

Storing and Retrieving Data
The basic task of Excel is data retrieval and storage (either numerical or text-based). Cells in an Excel spreadsheet are organized in a matrix with numbered columns and lettered rows.

Data Storage and Retrieval
Excel provides an efficient and effective method of saving large quantities of data.

Excel provides a helpful and effective structure for managing data. This apparently easy structure enables you to save large volumes of data, evaluate that data, and display the knowledge you gain in a diversity of ways. The original data is the integral part for each of these operations. The resulting evaluation or presentation is just as excellent as the data on which it was drawn. Excel is also not an issue of contention to the "garbage in, garbage out" concept that is applicable to several commercial applications, procedures, and systems.

How to Save in Excel

In order to reuse a workbook repeatedly after creating it, you have to save it. Also, you need to save a workbook whenever you make changes to it. Sometimes you could make a duplicate of a current workbook and also save it with a new title in a separate folder, or as a different kind of file.

Save a Workbook
Once you've created a new workbook, you'll need to save it if you want to use it again.

To Save a Workbook
To swiftly save a worksheet, click Ctrl + S.
Then, Save As screen would pop up when you're saving the workbook for the very first time.

How To Retrieve Data in Excel

Take a look at two situations in which you might want to retrieve your data:
1.   You are dealing with a fresh document but you've never saved it at all; or
2.   Before you can save the updates from your earlier save, the already saved document closes. Your documents could be recoverable in both instances; however, they'd be done in an entirely different manner.

To retrieve your never-before-saved document as described in the initial case stated above, open MS Excel first. Next press Open on the File tab of the Ribbon. At the bottom of the page, after choosing Recent, click Retrieve Unsaved Workbooks.

When your already saved document closes just before you are able to save the adjustments done since the previous save, you may have to retrieve the document. Start Excel once your system has normalized to regain the file.

All unsaved Excel files will be displayed in a Document Recovery box that appears. Select the file you would like to restore.

Using The Fill Handles

Fill Handle is a function in Excel that instantly fills the columns and rows according to the structure of values within specified cells and produces a list of series.

Each cell possesses an extremely small black box referred to as the fill handle which can be tapped on and dragged with the mouse, or double click to instantly fill the cells and generate a series of numbers based on the values that were inputted in the specified cells.

Depending on the value in the cell(s) in the starting cells from which you intend to build a list, the Fill Handle can be used to automatically fill the cells.

The approach for applying the Fill Handle to instantly fill the list using any type of value, such as dates, weekdays, numbers, and formulas, remains unchanged.

To Instantly Fill the Number Series Pattern via Drag and Drop, Use the Fill Handle.

To create a series, first insert a value in the cell you choose to start with. Then press and hold the Fill Handle and drag it up to the cell you want to replicate the series into.

Next, after opening the Fill Handle box and choose "Fill Series," your list will be transformed into the series with 1-increment

Rather, insert the value for at least 2 cells to build a structure that Fill Handle can adopt.

Then, once both cells have been chosen, set the mouse cursor on the cell's bottom right corner. An addition (+) symbol (Fill Handle) would then display.

Now, press and hold the mouse icon while dragging to the cell where you would like the sequence to instantly be filled.

Examining the Formulas All Simultaneously

Excel Formulas Cheat Sheet
Dates and Time Excel Formulas Cheat Sheet

=EDATE – In Excel, one could add a specific number of months to a date.

=EOMONTH – Convert a date (such as 5/10/2023 to 5/31/2023) to the last day of the month.

=DATE – Returns an integer depiction of the date (yyyy/mm/dd) in Excel. When employing Excel features that utilize a date as an argument, this formula is essential.
=TODAY – Input and present the current date in a cell.

=YEAR – Retrieves and presents the year in Excel from a date (for example, 3/12/2023 to 2023).

Navigation Excel Formulas Cheat Sheet
Navigate to Special - click F5 and search every cell which are formulas, formulas and more. Perfect for auditing

Find and Replace - By clicking Ctrl +F you can modify sections of various formula simultaneously.

Lookup Formulas
INDEX MATCH – a set of strong lookup operations combined with VLOOKUP

=VLOOKUP –a lookup function that searches a table vertically

=HLOOKUP – a lookup function that searches a table horizontally

=INDEX – a lookup function that browses horizontally and vertically in a table

=MATCH –returns a value's position within a series.

=OFFSET –adjusts a cell's reference by the given number of columns and/or rows

Leverage the Goal Seek Formula
A tool for what-if analysis is the Excel Goal Seek function. Goal Seek permits you to attain that aim by functioning backwards to arithmetically

change one specific variable inside the equation, provided you actually know the one result you'd like to accomplish.

Goal seek is commonly used in financial models, but it is also generally used in forecasts for elections, sales and other events.

We can define a desirable output via the use of Excel's Goal Seek command, which will work out what modification to apply to one particular variable. In order to determine the required income figure, we would employ Goal Seek.

Goal Seek in Excel, A pop-up window will show after selecting the Goal Seek command. Input the cell reference that will include the output you seek under "Set cell" (in this case, C14). Input the expected result (15%) in the "To value" field.
The third field, "By modifying cell," refers to the cell (C1) which you would want Excel to modify to generate the desired outcome.
When you choose OK, Excel will estimate the income needed to enable a 15% savings by working backward. The objective of goal seek is to arrive at an answer that perfectly matches the target value.

Automate Recurring Responsibilities With VBA

How To Use VBA (Visual Basic) Programming to Automate Tasks in Excel

Using VBA programming, you can absolutely manage very tedious operations.

You can simply alter a code to match whatever task you need to execute. Piece by piece, unraveling the programming renders it remarkably clear to comprehend.

Now let us look at an instance where VBA code can help simplify your work.

To employ the VBA coding, ensure the Developer feature is active in Excel. You must go to Excel > Preferences > Ribbon & Toolbar, choose Customize the Ribbon, and then enable the Developer option. Next you click on the Developer tab to access Macros.

You could record a macro, but you have to modify the coding if you want to "categorize" it to execute an operation, like, eighty times (without recording yourself going through the process eighty times!).

The Best Excel Template to Enhance or Improve Productivity

Applying templates in Microsoft Excel not only saves so much time but also improves performance. Working without bothering about the style of your worksheet, and save time through using templates instead of generating complex formulas from the start.

Every template can be modified and tailored to suit your demands. They have no fixed features; rather they just act as the foundation for your project.

Some Templates for Excel Productivity

1. Family Budget Planner

Excel Template for a Family Budget

This easy but highly helpful template keeps count of finances among your family or group. You may simply enhance your finances with the help of sections for, individual earning, spending, total income, and other sections.

2. Personal Budget Spreadsheet
Template for a Personal Budget Spreadsheet
Through the use of this personal budget, you could see your income, expenditures, and your savings potentials

3. Project Gantt Chart
Template for a project Gantt Chart
You get total control to properly oversee deliverables, resources, plans and thanks to this comprehensive and effective template. Use this Gantt chart template to keep records of every single deliverable for your task.

Chapter 6: Relative, Absolute and Mixed Cell References in Excel

Absolute, Relative, and Mixed Cell References in Excel
Cells comprises of an Excel spreadsheet. By defining the row value and the column value, these cells can be referenced to.
B2 could, for instance, refer to the second column (denoted as B) and the second row (designated as 2)

There are now three main types of cell references provided in Excel:
Absolute Cell References
Mixed Cell References
Relative Cell Reference

What are Relative Cell References in Excel?
Relative References
All cell references are all by default relative references. When replicated through numerous cells, they are altered in line to the connection between columns and rows. For instance, the formula =C1+D1 would yield =C2+D2 if you transfer it from row 1 to row 2. If you have to execute that very same calculation throughout many columns or rows, relative references are extremely helpful.

When to Use Relative Cell References in Excel
Relative cell references can be needed when you want to create a formula for a set of cells and the formula must be able to make a reference to a relative cell reference.
When this happens, you can develop the formula inside one cell and duplicate it before pasting it into any other cell.

What is Absolute Cell Reference in Excel?
When entering a cell, there could be instances that you don't want a cell reference to change. Absolute references don't change when duplicated or filled in, in contrast to relative references. To sustain the consistency of a column and/or row, apply an absolute reference.
In a formula, an absolute reference is specified by putting a dollar character ($) just before a row or column.

What Does the Dollar ($) Sign Do?

If the dollar character ($) is put before a column and row values, it becomes absolute (i.e., Prevents the column and row value from changing when duplicated to another cells).

For instance, if I duplicated the formula from cell A2 to cell A3, it would change to =C3*F1 rather than =C2*F1.

It is important to note that F1 stays unchanged while C2 was altered to C3.

As we placed a dollar ($) character in front of "F" and "1" in "F1," the cell reference cannot change when the cell was duplicated.

When to Use Absolute Cell References in Excel

Because you do not want the cell reference to be modified when you duplicate formulas, absolute cell references are helpful. This may be an issue if you have to use a fixed value within the formula (such as, number of months, commission rate, tax rate etc.)

What Are Mixed Cell References in Excel?

A relative reference and an absolute reference are both constituent of a mixed reference. This implies that a component of the reference, either the column or the row, is fixed, whereas the remaining portion is relative.

A mixed reference could be conveyed through any of the two ways:

=$B1 ($ preceding column, keeping the column's constant value)

=B$1 ($ in preceding the row and retaining the row's constant value)

How to Change the Reference from Relative to Absolute (or Mixed)?

To convert the reference from a relative to an absolute, the $ symbol should be added before the column notation and the row number.

For instance, the relative cell reference B1 would change to the absolute cell reference B1 when you altered it.

If you simply want to make a few modifications to these references, it could be easier to make the modifications manually. You could therefore modify the formula by navigating to the formula bar (rather choose the cell, click F2, and then alter it).

You could also execute this more quickly by pressing F4 on the keyboard. Clicking F4 alters the reference for the chosen cell if it's in an edit form or within the formula bar.

Create Multiplication Table in Excel and Google Sheets

Create Multiplication Table in Excel

Setting up Data

Input the numbers 1 to 10 in cells B2 through B11 and once again in cells C1 through L1 to set up the data.

Also, applying the TRANSPOSE function, it is another unique approach to input the numbers into the cells:

Insert the number 1 to 10 in cells B2-B11.

Insert the following formula in the formula bar after choosing the range B1:K1.

Given that the formula is an array, press Ctrl+Shift+Enter.

=TRANSPOSE(B2:B11)

You now have the multiplication table set up.

Mixed-reference multiplication table

The multiplication table can be created using mixed cell references, in which one column or row reference is fixed and the other is not.

Make use of this formula in cell C2:

=$B2*C$1

This will multiply the header column row and lock the header row for a particular number before giving the result.

Afterwards, we'll copy and paste the formula to the whole range:

Copy cell C2 (Ctrl + C).

choose the range C2:L11

Paste the formula using Ctrl+V

Setting up Data

Data Entry Form in Excel.

You may have observed that there is no option in Excel for creating a data entry form (not in any tab in the ribbon).

Before using it, you should first add it as part of the Quick Access Toolbar (or the Ribbon).

Use the following steps to add the data entry form option to the Quick Access Toolbar:

Right-click on one of the Quick Access Toolbar that is available.

Select "Customize Quick Access Toolbar" by clicking it. The Quick Access Toolbar option should be customized.

In the 'Excel Options' dialog box that opens, select the 'All Commands' option from the drop-down. Select All Commands from the drop down Choose "Form" among the menu of commands when you scroll down. On the Excel Options dialog box, you can choose the Form option. Select the "Add" button. Select the Add button. Choose OK.

How to Make Data Entry Form in Excel

A data entry form can only be added to an Excel table that is properly functioning. Simply input your data into a table and choose the Form icon to access the form. The precise steps are listed below:
Enter the column headings inside the top row of your spreadsheet as appropriate. Ignore this stage if you are inputting the form for an existing data set.
Using the Ctrl + T keys, select any cell in your dataset. This will choose every data element and transform it into a table.
Click the Form icon with the cursor in any part of the table.

Create The Multiplication Table in Google Sheets

Creating a formula in a worksheet cell is the simplest way to multiply two numbers in Google Sheets. The following are some essential criteria for Google Sheets formulas:
The equal sign (=) is often used to begin a formula.
In the cell where you expect the result to show, enter an equal symbol.
The asterisk (*) serves as the multiplication operator
The formula is done by hitting the Enter key on the keyboard.

Multiply Numbers in Google Sheets

Start Google Sheets and select an appropriate cell.
input the equal (=) sign.
input a number.
Google Sheets begins with a simple formula
Insert an asterisk (*) in front to denote multiplication.
Input the second value.
Google Sheets perform a simple formula
To see the answer, click Enter.

Numbering in Excel

If you have a number of items in Excel and you want to add a column that numbers the items, there are various approaches to achieve this. Let's now have a look at 3 of these approaches.

1. Use Auto-Fill to Create a Static List.

The first method for numbering a list is quite simple, you can start by inputting the first two numbers from your list, selecting these two numbers, and then moving your pointer over the selection's bottom right corner till it changes into a + symbol. This is the fill handle.

Excel will fill in the spaces with the subsequent number in the series if you double-click on the fill handle or drag it from the top to the bottom of your list.

2. Generate Dynamic List Using a Formula

The numbers in a dynamic list that change when you add or erase rows from the list can be created via formulas.

using a formula, you can apply the ROW function to produce a dynamic number list. The row number for a cell is given by ROW function. It simply returns the current row number that has been chosen when you do not indicate a cell for a ROW.

3. Build a Dynamic List Using a Formula in an Excel Table

The only change in the formula if we write the exact one yet using an Excel table is the fact that it will reference the column header as opposed to the absolute cell value.

How to Add a Serial Number Automatically in Excel.

Excel lacks a button to automatically number data, in contrast to other Microsoft 365 applications. But making use of the ROW function or sliding the fill handle to fill a column with a sequence of numbers, you might quickly add successive numbers into rows of data.

Insert a Number Sequence into a Column.

In the range you want to fill, choose the first cell.
The series' initial value should be inputted.
To create a trend, insert a value in the preceding cell.
To create the sequence 1,3,5,7,9, for instance, enter 1 and 3 into the first two cells.
Choose the cells which have the first values in them.
You can drag the fill handle over the range you intend to fill.
Excel presents a value sample when you slide the fill handle over every cell.
Drag the fill handle while still holding down the right -click button to select another design if you want.
Drag downward or towards the right to fill in the ascending order. Drag upwards or towards the left to fill in descending order.

Using the ROW Function to Number Rows

Enter =ROW(B2) in the first cell of the range you want to number
The number of the row you refer to is delivered by the ROW function. For instance, =ROW(B2) gives the value 2
You could fill a range by sliding the Fill handle over it.

Chapter 7: The WORKDAY.INTL Function

Depending on the offset value you provided, the Excel WORKDAY.INTL function reads a date and gives the closest working n days ahead or in the past. WORKDAY.INTL, in contrast to the WORKDAY function, enables you to select what days are presumed weekends (non-working days). Use the WORKDAY.INTL function to determine ship dates, completion dates, etc. that take non-working days into consideration.

The four arguments for the WORKDAY. INTL functions are start date, days, weekends, and holidays. A valid Excel date should be used for Start_date. The days argument is the length of days to move from start_date in the past or future, accounting for non-working days. To progress in time, use a positive number representing the days, and to return backwards, use a negative number.
The weekend argument, which is optional, indicates what day(s) of the week ought to be weekends and, hence, non-working days. Automatically, WORKDAY.INTL will take Saturday and Sunday to be non- working days.

Example
Holidays are all in D1:D3, the start date appears in B1, and the days were adjusted to 1.
=WORKDAY.INTL(B1,1) // default - excluding Saturday and Sunday
=WORKDAY.INTL(B1,1,11) // only omit Sunday

How To Use The WORKDAY.INTL In Excel

Formula
=WORKDAY.INTL(days, Start date, (weekend), and (holidays))
These respective arguments are employed by the function:
Start_date (required function) – This date denotes the start date.
Days (required function) – The number of working days to be assigned to the start date. A positive number will show us a date in the future, and a negative number will show us a past date.
Weekend (optional argument) –This outlines the weekends and the days that shouldn't be counted as days of work. Weekend is an integer or string that denotes the dates of weekends. The weekend days are specified by the weekend number values:

Weekend number   Weekend days

1	or omitted
	Saturday, Sunday
2	Sunday, Monday
3	Monday, Tuesday

Weekend string –The seven 0s and 1s in this succession, starting with Monday, signify the 7 days of the week. 0 indicates a weekday, and 1 indicates a non-working day. For instance:

"0000001" – Only Sunday is the weekend.

"0000111" – Friday, Saturdays and Sunday are weekends.

WORKDAY. INTL Errors

Workday.Intl Errors

The Excel Workday.Intl function's issue is more likely to be one of the following:

#NUM!

Occurs if one of the following are true:

The given start_date and the given argument days returns an invalid date

The [weekend] argument that was given has an invalid number.

#VALUE!   -

Occurs if any of the below statement are true:

Start_date or any of the variables in the [holidays] array provided are invalid dates;

The [weekend] argument that was given is an invalid text string.;

The day's argument provided is not numerical.

Mistake #Num

When a function or formula has numerical values that are invalid, Excel presents this as a problem.

This commonly occurs when you insert a numerical value using a data type or number format that the argument area of the formula does not support. For instance, because dollar signs are used as absolute reference marks and commas are used as argument spacers in formulas, you cannot enter a number such as $3,000 in monetary format. Input figures as unformatted numbers, such as 3000, to prevent the #NUM! error.

#Value Error

Excel's means of stating that, "The manner in which your formula is expressed needs to be changed. Or there is an issue with the cells you are making reference to." Because the issue is so broad, determining its specific root problem could be difficult.

MS Excel: The RANDBETWEEN Function

This function will give back a random integer number between the user-specified integers. Every time the worksheet is opened or a calculation is done, a random integer number will be returned.
Formula
=RANDBETWEEN (bottom, top)
The RANDBETWEEN function uses the following arguments:
Bottom (function is required) – This is the minimum number that the function would ever return.
Top (required function) – This is the maximum number that the function would return.

How to Use the RANDBETWEEN Function in Excel?

The RANDBETWEEN function could be used to produce randomly spaced integers that are uniformly distributed between a user-specified top and bottom range.
=RANDBETWEEN(bottom, top)
Enter the Arguments
bottom –The minimum number RANDBETWEEN will give.
top – The maximum number RANDBETWEEN will give.

Tips For the RANDBETWEEN Function

Comparable to the RAND function, the RANDBETWEEN function enables you to give a range of values, for instance, between 10 and 10,000 or 5 and 5000. The produced random numbers are best suited for the majority of circumstances provided the decimals in the RAND command have been erased. But, if you solely want four-digit or six-digit numbers, use RANDBETWEEN to select a number set that fits into that condition.

Excel RAND Function

RAND produces a randomly created real number higher than or equal to 0 and less than 1 that is dispersed equally. Every time the worksheet is calculated, a new random real number is produced.
RAND()
There are no arguments in the RAND function syntax.
Use this formula to create a random real number between c and d:

=RAND()*(d-c)+c

Create Random Numbers

A collection of random integers between two values you choose could be easily created. Additionally, you can create random decimal values or possibly a random list of all the numbers that range from 1 to 20.
To generate random numbers in Excel using RANDBETWEEN:
The cell wherein you want the first random number to display should be clicked.
Enter=RANDBETWEEN(2, 400) replace "2" for the minimum random number you want to get and "400" for the maximum.
A random value inside the range will be produced once you click enter.
You could fill in as many cells as you would like using the exact formula by pressing and holding the small square in the bottom edge of the cell and dragging downward.
Excel will regenerate the values each time you make a modification. If you want to retain the numbers exactly the same, copy and paste your formula as the values.

Chapter 8: The VLOOKUP Function

Excel VLOOKUP Function

In Excel, you'll find a designed function called VLOOKUP that permits searching throughout many columns.

It consists of these respective components and is typed =VLOOKUP:

=VLOOKUP(col_index_num, lookup_value, [range_lookup],table_array)

The column having the lookup data should be on the left.

The function's various sections are split by a symbol, which could be a comma or semicolon;

Your language choices will define the symbol.

Lookup_value:Choose the cell that the search values will be inputted.

Table_array:The whole table range, that contains every cell.

Col_index_num:The information being looked up. The column's number, counted from the left, is the input:

Range lookup: (1) if numbers, TRUE; otherwise, text (0).

How To Use the VLOOKUP Function.

Choose a cell (C4)

Enter =VLOOKUP

Double click on the VLOOKUP command.

Choose the cell that the lookup value would be inputted (C3)

Enter (,)

Specify the table range. (B2:F21)

Enter (,)

Counting from the left, insert the column's number. (2)

Enter True (1) or False (0) (1)

Click "Enter"

Enter a value in the cell selected for the Lookup_value C3(7)

Let's look at an instance!

To determine the Pokémon's names depending on each ID#, use the VLOOKUP function:

The search outcome is in C4. The Pokémon names in this instance depend on their ID numbers.

C3 had been specified as the lookup value. The searched keyword is typed in this cell. Here, this corresponds to the Pokémon's ID number.

The table's range is specified at table array, in this instance B2:F21

Col index number is given as 2, which is inserted. The data being looked up is in this column, that is the second column on the left.

Then, the value 1 (True) is typed in the range lookup section. It is possible because the leftmost column mainly includes numbers. If it contained text, the result could have been 0 (False).

The #N/A value is the value that the function shows. This is owing to the Search ID# C3 section having been left vacant.

when you input a value to it, enter C3(7):

The Pokémon Squirtle with ID# 7 will be successfully obtained via the VLOOKUP function.

Sort The Information

When you add more data to a worksheet, organizing the data becomes extremely important. Sorting your information enables you to swiftly rearrange a worksheet. A list of contact information, for instance, could be sorted by last name. There are various other methods to arrange content, in addition to numerical and alphabetical.

It's vital to determine whether you would like to sort data all through the full worksheet or simply within a specific cell range before starting.

Your worksheet's data is organized by one column via the sort sheet. Whenever the sort is used, similar data across each row is stored together. When dealing with a sheet that has multiple tables, sort range would be helpful since it sorts the data in a range of cells and other worksheet information will not be affected when sorting a range.

To sort a sheet

For instance, let's sort a T-shirt order form alphabetically by Last Name (Using any column).

choose the cell in the column you wish to sort by. e.g., cell D2.

To sort through A to Z or Z to A, select the Data tab on the Ribbon, and click between the A-Z or Z-A commands.

The selected column would be used to sort the worksheet. The worksheet in this case has been arranged by last name.

What to look up, Tell the function

What is the LOOKUP Function?

Lookup function is grouped under Reference functions and Excel LOOKUP. The Functions returns the correlating value from another one-row or one-column range after performing a roughly match lookup in a one-row or one-column range.

The LOOKUP function can be used in financial analysis to compare two rows or columns. It is built to perform the basic vertical and horizontal lookup cases.

Lookup is in two forms: Array and Vector formats.

In its vector format, the LOOKUP function will search one row or column of data for a particular value before getting the data in the exact same location in an adjacent column or row.

The function's formula is as follows:

=LOOKUP(lookup_value, lookup_vector, [result_vector])

The preceding arguments are used:

Lookup_value (required function) –This is the value in which we would search. This could relate to either a text, number, cell or have a logical value of TRUE or FALSE.

Lookup_vector (required function) – If you intend to search this one-dimensional set of data. keep in mind that you have to arrange the data in ascending order.

Result_vector –An optional one-dimensional list of data through which you want to get back a value. The [result vector], if given, must have the exact same size as the lookup vector. The result is delivered from the lookup vector if the [result vector] is left out.

The array form of LOOKUP searches the first column or row of an array for the specified value, returning a value in the same place in the last column or row of the array. When the values we intend to match are in the array's first column or row, we can apply this format of LOOKUP.

Formula (Array) LOOKUP Function

= LOOKUP(lookup_value, array)

These are the arguments:

Lookup_value (required argument) –This is the value we're looking for.

Array (required argument) –A collection of cells that we like to contrast with the lookup value and that include numbers, logical values, or text.

How to use the LOOKUP Function in Excel.

Tell The Function Where to Look

What is the COLUMN Function in Excel?

An Excel lookup/reference function is the COLUMN function. When getting and looking up the column number for a specific cell reference, this function is important. For instance, since column B is the second column, the expression =COLUMN(B10) yields 2.

Formula
=COLUMN([reference])

Reference is the sole argument employed by the COLUMN function, and it's an optional argument. This is a range of cells or cell that you need the column number for. The column number for a specific cell or set of cells are needed. We shall get a numeric value from the function.

Tell Excel What Column to Output the Data From

The column number of the given cell reference is given by the COLUMN function. For instance, since column D is the fourth column, the expression =COLUMN(D10) yields 4.

Syntax
COLUMN([reference])

The following argument is part of the COLUMN function syntax:

The COLUMN function gives back the column numbers of reference as a horizontal array when the reference argument is excluded or makes reference to a range of cells and if the COLUMN function is inputted as a horizontal array formula.

What is VLOOKUP?

VLOOKUP, commonly referred to as vertical lookup, is another Excel's commonly used function. It was built particularly to explore tables and database sources and to get data.

The function looks for a value in the table's first column and gives back a value on the same row in a specified column for doing vertical searching down that column.
=VLOOKUP(lookup_value, table_array, col_index_num, [range_lookup])
Lookup_value

the value to search up in the table's left-most column.
Table_array
The range of cells where data is given.
Col_index_num
The number of the table column in which the value that corresponds must
be returned. The very first column is number one, then by number two, and
so forth.
[Range_lookup]
It's optional. —it is not needed for input.

VLOOKUP In Financial Modeling and Financial Analysis

In financial modeling and many other forms of financial analysis,
VLOOKUP formulas are commonly applied to give models more character
and incorporate various possibilities.
Considering a financial model that includes a debt schedule and three
potential interest rate scenarios for the enterprise: 3.0%, 5.0%, and 7.0%. If
a lower, moderate, or higher scenario is found, a VLOOKUP can output
the matching interest rate into the financial model.

The HLOOKUP Function

The Excel function HLOOKUP refers to horizontal lookup. This function
tells Excel to check in a row (known as "table array") for a particular value
in order to collect a value from another row in the same column.
Excel's HLOOKUP function is comprised of 4 two sections:
The value you wanted to look up;
The value to be looked for as well as the returned value, in the range;
The number of the row that bears the returned value from within the range
you specified;
0 or FALSE for a perfect fit with the value you're searching for; 1 or TRUE
to indicate a near match
Syntax: HLOOKUP([value], [range], [row number], [false or true])

How To Use the HLOOKUP Functions in Excel

The syntax for the HLOOKUP function in Microsoft Excel is:

HLOOKUP(value, table, index_number, [approximate_match])
Arguments or Parameters
Value
The value to consider in the table's first row.

Table
A minimum of two rows of information organized in increasing order.

index_number
The table row number wherein the appropriate value should be returned.
The first row is one.

approximate_match
Optional. To get a perfect fit, input FALSE. To get an approximated fit,
input TRUE. TRUE is the automatic value if this option is left out.

Returns
The HLOOKUP function could yield any type of data, which include dates,
numbers, strings and more.
The HLOOKUP function will give back #N/A if the approximate match
option has been set to FALSE and no perfect match is detected.
The subsequent smaller value is yielded if the approximate match option is
specified as TRUE and no exact match is obtained.
The HLOOKUP function will give back #VALUE! if the index number is
less than 1.
The HLOOKUP function returns #REF! if the index number is higher
than the total number of columns in the table.

Tips For HLOOKUP Function

When you decide to look down a particular number of rows and your
comparable values are organized in a row throughout the top of a data
table, apply HLOOKUP. When your comparable values are in a column to
the left of the data you're searching for, use VLOOKUP.

The numbers that appear in the first row of the table array should be in
increasing order provided range lookup is TRUE: ...-3, -2, -1,0, 1, 2, 3..., A-
Z, FALSE, TRUE; else, HLOOKUP would not return the right result.
Table arrays may not be required to be sorted if range lookup returns
FALSE.

Text typed in lowercase or uppercase are equal.

Chapter 9: The TRANSPOSE function(ws)

What is the TRANSPOSE Function?

Transpose Function is grouped under Reference and Excel functions. This will alter the array or range's orientation. A horizontal range will be changed into a vertical range by using this function, and vice versa.

The TRANSPOSE function is crucial in financial analysis to organize data in the way they need it.

Formula
=TRANSPOSE(array)

There are a set of cells in the array argument. The first row of an array would become the first column of the new array, the second row would also become the second column of the new array, and so forth in order to generate the transposition of the array.

In order to insert an array formula in Excel, we must:

Outline the set of cells that makeup the function result

Press CTRL-SHIFT-Enter after putting the function in the first cell of the range.

How To Use the TRANSPOSE Function in Excel

Firstly, choose some vacant cells. But be certain you choose exactly the same number of cells in the opposite direction to the original collection of cells. For instance, consider these six vertically positioned cells (A, B, C, D, E, and F):

So, we would have to choose certain horizontal cells, as you can see below:

Cells A4:D6

The recently transposed cells would end up in this location.

Then, insert =TRANSPOSE(

Type =TRANSPOSE(when those empty cells are still highlighted.

The range of the original cells would be entered in the subsequent step.

Input the range of the cells you intend to transpose now. To transpose cells from A2 to B5 in this case, the formula would be: =TRANSPOSE(A2:B5) -- but don't click ENTER yet! Simply stop typing, and move to the next step.

Finally, enter CTRL+SHIFT+ENTER

Dynamic Array vs Traditional Array

Here are the most essential differences:

In one cell, a formula for a dynamic array is inputted, and it is finalized with the usual Enter keystroke. The traditional array formula is completed by pressing Ctrl + Shift + Enter.

New array formulas instantly spill to multiple cells. To yield many outputs, CSE formulae must be replicated to a range of cells.

As the data in the source range evolves, dynamic array formula' output instantly adjusts. As the data in the source range changes, the dynamic array formula automatically resizes the output. If the return area is too small, CSE formulas shorten the output, and if it is too large, errors are delivered in additional cells.

In one cell, a dynamic array formula is conveniently modifiable. You would choose and modify the complete range to alter a CSE formula.

In a CSE formula range, you would first clear each of the current formulas prior to being able to erase and enter rows. Putting or erasing rows is not a problem when using dynamic arrays.

Tips for the TRANSPOSE Function

The range is not necessary to be mechanically typed. You could apply your mouse to choose the range after entering =TRANSPOSE(. To move from the starting of the range to the ending, simply click and drag. Nevertheless, be mindful to press CTRL+SHIFT+ENTER instead of pressing ENTER when you are through.

Chapter 10: Excel Data Entry Form

Parts of the Data Entry Form

Most persons enter data into Excel spreadsheets in the customary way, cell by cell and row by row. You can apply a specialized data entry form to accelerate and make the operation more user-friendly. Without navigating horizontally across columns, it will make it less difficult for you to stay focused on one record at a time.

Excel contains a specialized format for inputting data into spreadsheets that accelerates the procedure, simplifies it for users to use, and minimizes the possibility of errors—especially in large worksheets.

How To Add the Form Tool to Excel

All editions of Excel from 2007 to 365 contain the Form tool, but by design it is disabled and thereby, you should first keep it accessible via including the Form button on the Quick Access Toolbar, the Ribbon, or both.

The following are the processes to follow in order to add the Form tool to the Quick Access Toolbar (QAT):

Choose the small arrow button at the far-right of the QAT, and then select Extra Commands in the pop-up option. Command being added to the Quick Access Toolbar.

Select All Commands or Commands not found on the Ribbon under Choose commands form in the Excel Options dialog box that displays. Once you locate Form, navigate through the list of commands on the left and choose it.

To join the Form to the list of QAT commands on the right, hit the Add icon in the center.

To save the changes and end the dialog, select OK. The form button should be added to the QAT.

The Form button will be visible across all of your workbooks and will be readily accessible on your Quick Access Toolbar. The Quick Access Toolbar will now have the Form button.

As the Form tool is enabled in Excel, all it takes to generate a data entry form for any table—new or old—is a one button tap.

How To Make Data Entry Form in Excel

Just a fully functional Excel table can have a data entry form. Just input your relevant data in a table and choose the Form icon to access the form. Below are the precise procedures:

Insert the column headings in the top row of your spreadsheet as appropriate. Avoid this stage if you're creating an entry form for an existing data collection.

Press the Ctrl + T buttons concurrently when choosing any cell in your dataset. This would choose each set of data and transform it into a table. Everywhere inside the table, put the pointer, and choose the Form icon.

How To Add a New Record

Employ the data entry form to add a fresh record to your table by following these steps:

Choose any cell in your table.

In the Quick Access Toolbar or the ribbon, select the Form button.

Select the New icon on the entry form.

Enter the Data in applicable areas

Once you are done, click the Enter key or select the New icon once more. This will create the record for the table and give an empty form for the subsequent record.

Navigating Through the Existing Records

These are Four quick Excel tips for making data navigation quicker:

NOTE: THE KEYBOARD SHORTCUTS KEYS STATED HERE WORK WITH WINDOWS OPERATIONAL SYSTEMS.

1. **Transiting to a dataset's terminal column or row**

CTRL + down arrow/Up arrow/right arrow/left arrow

If you have ever had to go over a dataset with many rows and columns, you could have done it via the arrow keys on your keyboard or the scroll bars on the bottom or side of the screen in order to reach the final row or column.

2. **Moving to other tabs in the workbook**

Click CTRL + Page up/Page down for Windows with full keyboard

Click CTRL + fn + up arrow/down arrow for Windows with most laptops

By clicking CTRL + Page Up or CTRL + Page Down on your keyboard, you can rapidly shift between tabs to the right or left of the one you're on.

3. **Selecting/highlighting many cells**

SHIFT + arrows

Simply hold down the shift key when using arrow keys to choose the cells you would like to select as a group. Use this in combination with method #1 (CTRL + SHIFT + arrow key) to choose all neighboring cells in a row or column.

4. **Selecting or Highlighting the Complete Row or Column**

Click shift + space bar to highlight the entire row

Click CTRL + spacebar to highlight the entire column
Using these shortcuts to be sure that each and every cell in that column or row is styled when you want to outline a complete column or row, for example, to modify the font or font size.

Deleting a Record

You should first properly select those rows if you intend to delete several rows instantly depending on the cell value they contain.
You have two alternatives for choosing the rows: either highlight the nearby cells that include the appropriate values and click Shift + Space, or select the needed non-adjacent cells while pressing the Ctrl key.
Besides that, you could use the row number icons to choose the entire lines. The number of the selected rows is shown adjacent to the end button. With an Excel "delete row" shortcut, you could instantly delete the appropriate rows after choosing each.

Remove Rows from The Entire Table

Having the delete row shortcut, you can simply delete rows out of a standard Excel list without adding any extra data to the right with two simple steps:
Specify the rows you would like to remove.
Apply the hotkey Ctrl + - (minus on the standard keyboard).
In a few seconds, the blank rows would be erased.

How To Quest for Records

You can scroll across table records in Excel 2010 tables via a data form or keystrokes till you locate the record you would want to modify or remove. You can check up a record in broader tables through the search criteria in the data form. These procedures are compatible with conventional data collections that had not been changed into tables using the Table icon on the Insert tab.

How To Find Records in a Table Manually

The Quick Access toolbar setting in the Excel Options dialog box can be used to add the Form icon, which reveals a data form, although it is not available on the Excel 2010 Ribbon. To explore the records in the data form, simply click the Form button on the Quick Access toolbar.

Next record: Click the down arrow key, Enter, Find Next icon, rather just select the down arrow at the bottom of the scroll bar.

Previous record: You could make use of the up-arrow key, Shift+Enter, then Navigate to the Previous button, or the up arrow at the top of the scroll bar.

First record: Click Ctrl+up-arrow key, click Ctrl+PgUp, or drag the scroll box to the top of the scroll bar

New, blank data form: Click Ctrl+down arrow key, click Ctrl+PgDn, or rather drag the scroll box to the bottom of the scroll bar

How To Use Search Criteria to Find Table Records

Use the Criteria button in the data form to search records in large Excel tables. Execute the following steps:

To enter the data form, select the Form icon on the Quick Access toolbar. Do not ignore to include this icon in the Quick Access toolbar.

In the data form, select the Criteria icon.

In an attempt to input the search criteria inside the vacant text boxes, Excel erases all the field entries in the data form and switches the record number with the phrase Criteria.

Input Criteria in One Or More Sections of The Data Form

Along with text and values, you can also use comparison operators like < and >= and wildcards like ? and * for both single and multiple characters respectively.

To access a record in a staff table, for instance, you could write D* in the Last Name column and Dublin in the Location field if you know the person's last name starts with D and they are located in Dublin.

Use the Criteria button to perform a record search with given information. Either choose the Find Previous or Find Next button.

The very first record that meets the required criteria is located by Excel.

Until you discover the appropriate record, go over this process as necessary.

How To Update and Restore Records

You can continuously save versions of your file while you operate on it if the AutoRecover setting is activated. The time you saved information will dictate how you recover it.

If You Have Saved the File

Enter the document you were working with.

Navigate to File then Info.

Choose the indicated document under Manage Workbook or Manage Presentation (when I closed without saving).

To update any already saved versions, choose Restore from the menu located at the top of the file.

If You Haven't Saved the File

To restore unsaved Excel workbooks, navigate to File then the Info next move to Manage Document.

Choose Open after selecting the document.

To save the file, choose Save by clicking the bar at the file's top.

Update a Record

You could modify a record's data while viewing it; afterwards, select the Update button to duplicate the changes to the database.

You might alter the order quantity, for instance, if you found a mistake in it. The Input sheet's Total formula would instantly recalculate to reflect the updated amount.

Select the Update icon once you're through updating the record to view the modified information in that record on the database sheet

How To Use the Data Validation Along with The Data Entry form

What Is Data Validation in Excel?

Excel uses a technique known as data validation to limit user input in a spreadsheet. There are 8 possible options for user input validation:

The validation criteria are put on the settings tab, and there are 8 ways for user input validation:

Any Value -Any recent data validation is erased.

Whole Number -It only takes whole numbers. You might define that the user must enter a value between 0 and 20, for example.

Decimal - A number with decimal values should be inserted by the user.

List -A drop-down list for the user to select from must be created.

Date - The date format should be specified by the user.

Time -The user must input a time.

Text Length - It validates input depending on how lengthy the data is.

Custom - It makes use of a special formula to validate the user entry.

How To Validate Data in Excel?

Step 1 - Choose the Cell for Validation

Choose the cell you need to validate and move to the Data tab>Data tools, then click on the Data Validation icon.

A data validation dialog box with 3 tabs—Settings, Input Message, and Error Notifications will show up.

Step 2 - Specify Validation Criteria

You could set your validation criteria on the settings tab.

Step 3 - Under Allow, Choose the Criteria

Under Allow Choose from Text Length, Whole Number, Time, Date, List, Custom, Decimal.

Step 4 - Select Condition

According to the criteria you define for Allow and Data, choose a condition under Data and specify the appropriate values.

Step 5 - Input Message

If you wish, you might insert the entry text. This step is not necessary.

Step 6 - Custom Error Message

Moreover, you could define a customized error message. This step is not necessary.

Step 7 - Click Ok

Select OK. So, if you try to type in a value that goes beyond the designated range, an error will result.

Formulas in Data entry

Data Entry Shortcuts

Here are some time-saving Microsoft Excel shortcuts to use when you're entering data.

Keyboard Shortcuts

Ctrl + ; to enter the current date

Ctrl + Shift + ; enter to determine the present time

Enter Data in Multiple Cells

Choose every cell you want to enter a formula or value into

Enter into the active cell with both the formula or value.

Hold the Ctrl key and press Enter

Chapter 11: Excel Valuation Modeling

What is Valuation Modeling in Excel?
So many kinds of analysis, such as comparable trading multiples, precedent transactions, discounted cash flow (DCF) analysis, and ratios like horizontal and vertical analysis, are all defined by the term "valuation modeling" in Excel. The several kinds of analyses might be developed completely from start in Excel or could employ a template or format which already exists. Different kinds of finance experts often carried this kind of work.

Why Perform Valuation Modeling in Excel?
Excel valuation modeling can be conducted for a number of reasons, and specialists within a diverse set of industries invest a considerable amount of time performing this sort of task. Among the reasons are:
Organizational succession planning
For internal planning and budgeting
Getting prepared to seek funds investor (i.e., Determining what price shares should be issued at)
Determining the pricing range to consider while selling a business
Analyze prospective investments and capital projects
For assigning shares to staffs (an Employee Share Ownership Plan or ESOP)
Evaluate investment opportunities and capital projects

How to perform valuation modeling in Excel?
There are 3 major ways to value a firm, as formerly stated above. The most comprehensive method—discounted cash flow, or DCF—analysis is generally the one that is depended upon. An overview of each style of modeling is given below.

1 Discounted Cash Flow Modeling in Excel
Using the DCF process, a finance specialist develops an Excel model using between three- and five-years' amounts of historical financial data on an organization. The three financial statements are therefore merged in a flexible manner by a bridge.
After that, forecasts for the future are generated through Excel formulas using assumptions about how the company will operate in the future (typically, about five years into the future). Lastly, they measure the

business' terminal value and, through using company's Weighted Average Cost of Capital (WACC), discount both the predicted period and the maturity value back to the present.

2 Comparable trading multiples in Excel
Excel's comparable multiples valuation modeling approach varies substantially from a DCF model's approach. With this method, instead of determining a company's actual value, an analyst will analyze the valuation multiples of numerous other publicly traded organizations and compare them to those of the business(es) they would like to evaluate. The valuation multiples,EV/EBIT,EV/EBITDA,Price/Book,Price/Earnings,EV/Revenue and are typical examples.

3 Precedent transaction modeling in Excel
An analyst will evaluate the prices paid for merger and acquisition (M&A) of related businesses that had previously taken place using this third method of valuation modeling in Excel. This is a comparative type of valuation as well, but unlike comparable trading multiples, these transactions are established in the past and include takeover premiums (the control value) (Which can swiftly become obsolete).

How to Execute Excel Valuation Modeling?

Planning Your Model
1. Specify the targeted outcome of the model.
2. Know the timeframes for both the model's development and its functional life.
3. Set the ideal trade-off for both "reusability" and "detail."

Discounted Cash Flow Modeling in Excel
Presently, organizations commonly adopt Excel's DCF model. Moreover, have you ever thought about what the current value of investments that will generate for you a particular rate of profit in the future could be? The current value of your investments will be established via discounted cash flow calculations. You can execute financial modeling of an organization through DCF valuations.
One of the most efficient tools a corporation has for determining its worth is the discounted cash flow model. It evaluates the value of an organization by discounting the prospective cash flow it might provide

Advantages of DCF Model

Below is a listing of the benefits of using the Excel DCF model;

1. The discounted cash flow calculation technique is very comprehensive.
2. Plays an essential role in determining intrinsic value
3. You do not have to make comparisons between the DCF value and the others after you 've calculated it using Excel.
4. A major tool for acquisitions and mergers is the DCF model.
5. Excel enables the DCF valuations simply to perform.
6. You can do a sensitivity analysis via a DCF model. The analysts are helped by understanding which investment assumptions could have a significant impact on the investment's future value.

Disadvantages Of DCF Model

Below is a listing of the benefits of making use of DCF model in Excel;

1. It can at times be tough to apply the DCF model. Data for DCF analysis is extremely challenging to get through. Consequently, this method can be challenging to determine.
2.Oftentimes DCF's calculations will vary in comparison to its counterparts. This indicates that the market variables are not included in the DCF model's evaluation. This will certainly lead to poor conclusions.

Equivalent Trading Multiples in Excel

A sort of financial index used in company valuation is known as trading multiple. Everyone adopts the most commonly accepted method of valuation when estimating the value of an organization, Discounted Cash Flow (DCF), though it's essential for bankers and buyers to examine how the market considers a specific stock within an industry with a corresponding market and the asset type. As a result, "Trading Multiples" are factored in, and the relative valuation is determined.

To know how related organizations are valued by the stock market as a multiple of Revenue, Earnings Per Share, EBIT, EBITDA etc. Traders apply trading multiples. The essential concept of comparison is the assumption that the stock markets are productive.

Precedent Transaction Modeling in Excel

Precedent Transaction Analysis

One of the "Big Three" valuation methods is the precedent transaction analysis, along with comparable company analysis and the DCF Model. Of these three methodologies, it is also the most "optional" or "supplemental" one.

It is hard to identify antecedent transactions and collect the information needed if you do n't get access to a costly subscription service like FactSet or Capital IQ.

Although one can have access to all the data and these resources, the analysis itself has the propensity to give outcomes which are more inconsistent and have a broader range of values than those produced by the other methods.

Jobs that Perform Valuation Modeling in Excel

1. Project Finance
2. Real Estate
3. Financial Planning and Analysis
4. Credit Analyst
5. Consultancy Firms
6. Corporate Finance
7. Equity Research Analyst
8. Financial Analyst
9. Investment Banking

Chapter 12: Excel math functions

MATHEMATICAL & STATISTICAL FUNCTIONS

Excel functions could likewise be used to do arithmetic operations in addition to formulas. A mathematical operation is used on a collection of cells in a worksheet by statistical functions. The SUM function, for instance, is used to add the values in a set of cells. The frequently used statistical functions are listed below. When performing a mathematical operation on a collection of cells, functions are more efficient than formulae.

Frequently Used Math Functions

ABS
It gives a number's exact value

AVERAGE
A set of numbers' arithmetic mean or average

COUNT
The number of numerical character-containing cell positions in a range

COUNTA
The number of numeric character or text places in a range of cells

MAX
The maximum numerical value in a number collection

MEDIAN
The central number within a set of numbers (Half of the range's numbers are higher than the median, and the other half are lesser than the median.)

MIN
The least number in a set of numbers

MODE
The number in a set of numbers that occurs often the most

PRODUCT
The outcome of multiplying all the variables in a set of cell positions

SQRT
The number's positive square root

STDEV.S
The sample-based standard deviation for a collection of numbers
SUM
A group's summation of all numerical values

Statistical Functions in Excel

Basic Statistical Functions in Excel

1. Count Function
Whenever you need to count the number of cells which include a number, simply use the count function. Bear in mind Just NUMBERS!

2. Counta Function
The COUNTA function counts each cell in a range that is not vacant, contrary to the count function, which strictly counts numerical values. The function could be applied to count cells regardless of the data, such as erroneous values and vacant text.

3. Countblank
In a cell range, the COUNTBLANK function estimates the number of vacant cells. The cells with empty text-returning formulas are also counted, but cells with zero values are not counted. This is an excellent feature to summarize empty cells while evaluating any data.

4. Countifs Function
One of the most commonly applied statistical functions in Excel is the countif function. The COUNTIFS function adds 1 or more criteria to the cells in the specified range and delivers just those cells that meet all of the requirements.

5. Average Function
The mean is the most often utilized function in our daily lives (or Average). The arithmetic mean of all the cells in a particular range is the value that the AVERAGE function basically gives:

6. Median Function

The application of the median, a distinct function for the central tendency, could be employed to fix the outliers. The median function gives a number that lies in the center of the selected cell range.

7. Mode Function

The mean and median are typically appropriate for numerical numbers, however how about categorical values? Mode comes into play in this case. In the provided set of values, mode delivers the one that is repeated and employed the most:

8. Standard Deviation Function

One method for determining dispersion is through standard deviation. It is a metric of the extent to which values deviate from the mean.

Excel Financial Function

Financial functions (reference)

EFFECT function
Delivers the actual yearly interest rate.

FV function
Delivers the investment's potential value

FVSCHEDULE function
Offers the value of an initial principal in the future after implementing various compound interest rates.

IPMT function
Returns the interest collected for a specific time frame on an investment.

IRR function
for a succession of cash flows, yields the internal rate of return.

ISPMT function
calculates the interest paid on an investment for a particular duration.

MIRR function
returns the internal rate of return in the scenario of various rates of financing for both positive and negative cash flows.

NOMINAL function

Delivers the nominal interest rate for the year.

NPER function
provides a number of investment durations.

NPV function
returns the investment's net present value using a set of consecutive cash flows and a discount rate.

Excel Text Functions (String function)

TEXT function
Through using format codes to add formatting to a number, you can modify how it looks while using the TEXT function. It can be helpful when you intend to join figures with text or icons or show numbers in a more comprehensible style.

The TEXT function states this in its most simple form:

=TEXT(Data that you want to format, "The format code you intend to use")

Here are some examples;

Formula

Description

=TEXT(TODAY(),"MM/DD/YY")
Date for today in an MM/DD/YY format, for instance 03/14/12

=TEXT(TODAY(),"DDDD")
Today's day of the week, such as Tuesday

=TEXT(0.285,"0.0%")

%, such as 28.5%

Logical Functions in Excel

Excel logical functions

To deal with the logical values, MS Excel features 4 logical functions. The operations are XOR, AND, OR, and, NOT. If you want to do many comparisons in your computation or test different criteria in contrast to a single one, you use these functions. Along with logical operators, Excel logical functions yield either TRUE or FALSE when their variables are evaluated.

Function
AND

If every variable equates to TRUE, this function yields TRUE. =AND(C2>=12, D2<6) If the value in cell C2 is more than or equivalent to 12 and the value in cell D2 is lesser than 6, the formula yields TRUE, else it yields FALSE.

OR

If any parameter is verified as TRUE, it delivers TRUE. =OR(C2>=12, D2<6) When either C2 is greater than or equivalent to 12 or D2 is lesser than 6, and otherwise if both criteria are fulfilled, the formula gives TRUE. If it did not satisfy any of the criteria it met, the formula gives FALSE.

XOR

Delivers a logical Exclusive or of all parameters. =XOR(C2>=12, D2<6) If either C2 or D2 has a value greater than or equivalent to 10 or lesser than 5, the formula gives TRUE. The formula delivers FALSE when either one or both of the criteria are true.

NOT

Delivers the parameter's logical value in opposite. That is, TRUE is delivered if the parameter is FALSE, and vice versa. =NOT(C2>=10) If a number in cell C1 has a value greater than or equivalent to 10, the formula yields FALSE; otherwise, it delivers TRUE.

In addition to the four logical functions outlined above, Microsoft Excel provides 3 "conditional" functions - IF, IFERROR and IFNA.

Chapter 13: Excel Table

What is an Excel Table?
Your data is housed in Excel Tables.
Excel is notified by tables that all the data is correlated. Only one relationship between the data outside a table is their closeness with respect to one another.

The Parts of a Table

The Column Header Row.
The column titles that indicate each row of a table's first column are located therein. The table's column headers must be different from one another, can't be vacant, and they can't have formulas in them.

The Body of the table.
The body serves as the place where all formulas and data are kept. This is a single table's rows. One or many rows could be present in a table's body, and when all the rows are intended to be removed, a blank row will remain.

The Column in the table.
A table should have one or more columns.

How To Create a Table in Excel

Create a Table from The Ribbon
Excel Table construction is very simple. Excel will determine the range of your data for building the table provided you select any cell inside your data. Later on, you'll be capable of verifying this range. You can optionally choose the complete range of data in this process other than having Excel try to determine the range.

Navigate to the Insert button on the ribbon and select the Table icon in the Tables section when your active cell is within your data range.
The dialog box for generating tables would display. With the range selector icon on the right side of the Where is the data for your table? entry section, you can modify Excel's recommended range if desired. By individually typing across the range in the entry section, you could also alter this range.

Whenever the box labeled "My table has headers" is selected, Excel is notified that the first row of data in your table will have the column headers. Unchecking this will allow Excel to build a nonspecific column. Navigate to the Insert tab on the ribbon and select the Table button in the Tables section when your active cell is inside your data range.

If you're convinced with the data range and table headers check box, select OK.

Create a Table with a Keyboard Shortcut

You can also create a table using a keyboard shortcut. The process is the same as described above but instead of using the Table button in the ribbon you can press Ctrl + T on your keyboard.

How To Make a Table with a Selected Style

Excel tables provide a variety of unique features, including computed columns, total row, integrated filter, sort options, structured references, etc., that significantly enhance accessing and managing data.

You could begin the formatting procedure by transforming the data to an Excel table. A newly entered table comes already formatted with borders, banded rows, font and background colors, and so forth. By choosing one of the built-in Table Designs on the Design page, you can instantly modify the conventional table format if you do not want it.

The location to begin while working with Excel table styles is the Design tab. Once you select any table cell, it displays in the contextual tab for Table Tools.

How To Select a Table Style When Building a Table

Do the following to format a table in a particular way:

Choose the collection of cells you want to transform into a table form.

Select Format as Table from the Styles group on the Home menu.

Selecting a table's style whenever you are developing a table

Select the style you intend on employing by clicking it in the Table Styles gallery.

How To Change Table Style in Excel

To apply a different style to an existing table, perform these steps:

To alter a cell's style inside the table, select it.

To display every Excel Table styles which are accessible, select the More button underneath the Table Styles section on the Design tab.

Excel will offer a live glimpse once you hover your mouse pointer over the style you want to select. Simply select the new style to use.

Delete all formatting and add a new table style.

How To Name a Table in Excel?

When you set up a table, Excel immediately gives it a default name that fits this naming scheme: Table1, Table2, Table3, and so on. You can give each table a title to make it simpler to reference it, for instance, in a workbook with multiple tables.

To Rename a Table:

Select The Table.

To locate the table name, navigate to Table Tools > Design > Properties.

Go to the Table tab > Table Name on a Mac.

Insert a different name after highlighting the table name.

How To Use Table in Excel

Working Efficiently With your Table Data

Excel contains a few capabilities that makes it easy to organize your table data successfully:

Using structured references

Structured references, which refers to table names in a formula, could be applied in lieu of cell references like B1 and H1D1.

Ensuring data integrity

Excel contains a built-in data validation function that you can employ. For instance, you might consider to confine the contents of a table column to only figures or dates.

How To Sort a Table in Excel?

Below are steps you can use to sort tables in Excel:

1. Choose a cell inside the data

Choosing a cell inside the data in a table is the starting point in filtering the data. Choose any cell in the data if you have a previously created table. You can construct a table if you haven't already done so. Any data value inside the table could therefore be selected to begin sorting once it has been created.

2. Go to your filter options

The sorting and filtering features are available in 2 distinct ways. You could access an options menu by selecting the "Sort & Filter" button which is located at the top of the "Home" tab. Alternatively, you can reach the menu of options by choosing the "Data" tab and look for the "Sort" button.

3. Choose a filter option

Excel offers 2 designed alternatives for sorting data in tables: "Sort A to Z" and "Sort Z to A," which alphabetically organize the data in the table. If neither of these choices matches to the way you would like the table to be sorted, select "Custom Sort" to build your own parameters. The steps seen below can be utilized, for instance, to sort data:

CHOOSE "Add Level"
Select "Column," "order," or "Sort on" from the alternatives.
Choose option from the drop-down menu after choosing "Sort by"
If you would like to sort your table with multiple criteria, apply "Then by."
To enable your table to use headers, choose the "My table has headers" option.
To enable Excel to sort the table, click "OK."

Excel Table Formulas

Create and Apply Formulas to Tables in Excel

Anywhere you would like the formula, enter an equal sign.
Because a table is being used, we refer to the columns in a new way.
Once you enter [, Excel offers a list of the table columns which you can use in your formula.
(Always commence and conclude a table reference by an open bracket and a closing bracket. [ ])

The complete column of data can be chosen by clicking one of the drop-down options, inputting the column name, or by entering the @ symbol preceded by the column name if you only want to refer to the current row. A closing bracket should be included after the name of the column as well. As soon as you click Enter, the formula will instantly duplicate the whole table down.

The solely required step is to use the necessary formatting.

How To Extend a Table in Excel

Resize A Table by Adding or Removing Rows and Columns

You could swiftly add or remove table columns and rows after building an Excel table in your worksheet.

To add columns and rows to a table in Excel, use the Resize command:

The Table Tools option shows when you click any area of the table.

Select Resize Table Underneath Design.

Applying the Table Tools resize table option

Beginning with the upper-left cell, choose the full range of cells you want your table to cover.

How to Remove the Table formatting

This is the procedure to follow in order to get rid of formatting yet keeping an Excel table's remaining features:

Choose any cell within your table.

Select the initial style in the Light group, which is termed None, underneath the Table Design tab of the Table Styles group.

In Excel, delete table formatting. Alternatively, select the Table Styles group, tap More, and then choose the Clear icon to the right of the table styles.

As a result, you continue to have an Excel table that is completely functional but without formatting.

How to Remove a Table in Excel?

This is how to erase the whole table if your Excel worksheet has data in a table format and you no longer need the data or its formatting. Choose Clear All from the Clear menu after selecting each cell in the table.

To remove a table, choose the clear all button on the ribbon.

Conclusion

You can modify, organize, and analyze data with MS Excel, which can support choice and offer effectiveness which will significantly impact your bottom line. Microsoft Excel offers you with the needed features to satisfy all of your requirements, either you 're using it for a job role or to help manage personal databases and expenditures.

With the assistance of Microsoft Excel's extensive analytical features, you could evaluate a lot of data to determine trends and patterns that will affect your decisions. You could summarize your data using graphical functions of MS Excel, this improves your capacity to organize and manage your data. Excel's spreadsheet has lately experienced changes that make it easier for you to examine incredibly huge portions of data.

Through the usages of advanced sorting, filtering, and search features, you may rapidly and conveniently reduce the number of choices that will affect your selections.

END

Thank you for reading my book.

Warren G. Garcia